CHIP
the
BUFFALO
based on a true story

by Cheri Lawson

To Bud, Dot, and
my grandchildren.

Photos courtesy of B&B Buffalo Ranch
by Tammy Beerntsen
Illustrations by J. Lawson

LUMINARY
Media Group
Published by Luminary Media Group,
an imprint of Pine Orchard, Inc.
www.pineorchard.com

2nd printing, 2007
Printed in Hong Kong

ISBN 1-930580-61-4
EAN 9781930580619

Library of Congress Control Number:
2006926641

"Spring-o-year, spring-o-year," sings a meadowlark from the top of a fence post. Clint enjoys the sweet sound of the songbird as he slowly drives his pickup truck in the field. He raises buffalo on his Montana ranch and it is calving time. Buffalo cows try to keep their new babies hidden from enemies. He carefully looks for calves around the sagebrush and under the tall pine trees.

1

At the top of a hill, Clint sees a newborn calf standing alone. He checks all the cows, but he cannot find the mother. "I'll find someone to take care of you," says Clint to the motherless calf. He gently picks up the red-haired calf and carries it to his truck. Back to the ranch house he goes . . . with the baby buffalo riding safely inside.

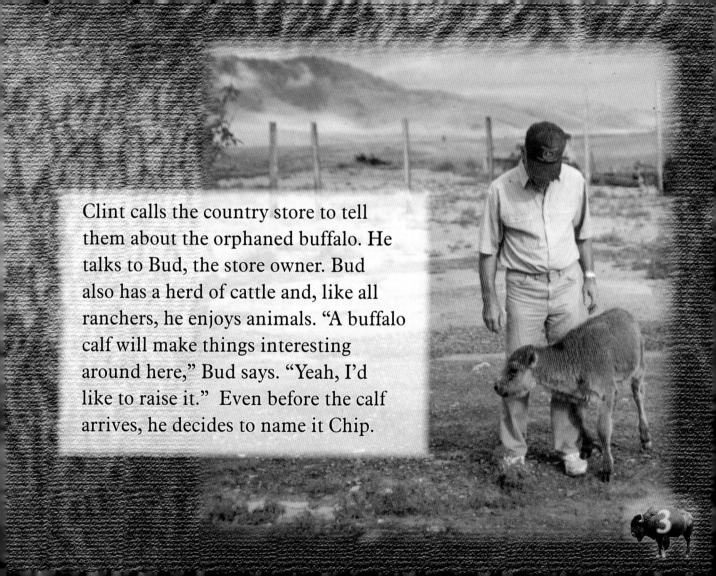

Clint calls the country store to tell them about the orphaned buffalo. He talks to Bud, the store owner. Bud also has a herd of cattle and, like all ranchers, he enjoys animals. "A buffalo calf will make things interesting around here," Bud says. "Yeah, I'd like to raise it." Even before the calf arrives, he decides to name it Chip.

3

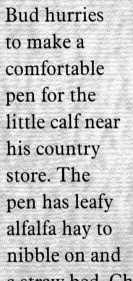

Bud hurries to make a comfortable pen for the little calf near his country store. The pen has leafy alfalfa hay to nibble on and a straw bed. Chip is a baby and needs to be bottle-fed. Bud stirs together powdered milk and warm water until all the lumps disappear. Then he pours the rich milk into a half-gallon bottle and goes to feed his hungry buffalo calf.

Feeding the buffalo is fun for everyone. Chip quickly gulps down the bottle of milk. Little milk bubbles foam around her mouth as she drinks. When the bottle is empty, she grunts *uh-uh* as if to say "thank you." Customers at the store have fun making the sound of a buffalo. They grunt back *uh-uh*.

During the day, Chip spends most of her time outside the pen. The paved parking lot turns into a little buffalo playground for her. One day, a local customer holds the store door open. "*Uh-uh*," the customer coaxes. "Come on inside, little girl."

Chip carefully inches her way onto the shiny floor. The other customers laugh with excitement when the baby buffalo stands by the candy counter. Bud fixes a bottle of milk and the frisky calf follows him back out the door. She playfully races around the gas pumps. Then she runs to get her dinner of milk.

7

Chip is growing big and strong. She no longer looks like a baby buffalo. Her fine red hair has turned to a coarse brown, almost a wooly texture. "A big buffalo calf running around the store might scare the customers," Bud decides. "She needs to wear a halter outside the pen." Now he leads Chip around with a rope tied to her new halter.

Slowly, Chip is weaned from the bottle. The feedings are cut back to three bottles a day . . . then two bottles a day . . . then one bottle a day . . . then none. She starts to eat pellets by the handfuls. The tasty little pellets are packed full of healthy things like vitamins and minerals, and are sweetened with molasses.

Chip is the center of attention at the country store. Customers are always happy to see the tame buffalo. Clint cares about the buffalo and stops in to see her often. Bud cares about the buffalo, too, and has grown attached to her. "I'm going to sell my cattle and raise buffalo," he decides.

The warm spring weather feels good to Chip. She is one year old and always ready to run free without a halter. Every morning, Bud takes her out of the pen for some exercise. She chases after the jeep as he drives to the corral.

Bitterroot plants are blooming in the dry fields around the corral. Chip puts her head down near the pink wildflowers and snorts. Suddenly, she hears a noise coming from inside the corral. Bud has a new herd of buffalo in the big pen. The restless buffalo look for a way to get out. They go around and around, snort and paw, snort and paw, snort and paw.

It takes a few days for the new buffalo to finally settle down. Then Bud turns them out to graze in the pasture. Chip is now a young cow and big enough to join the herd. Bud sadly puts her in the same field with the new buffalo. The sudden changes seem hard for her to understand.

She lies down on the ground when the curious buffalo circle around her. A killdeer also notices Chip and flutters its wings. "Kill-dee-dee," the bird sings. It probably has a nest of eggs nearby and is trying to lure the buffalo away. Chip pays no attention to the noisy bird.

13

Chip is unhappy living in the buffalo herd. The strange animals have a sweaty, musty odor. She can smell them from far away. The older bulls are huge and unfriendly. Most of the time they stay by themselves instead of with the herd. Chip also likes to stay by herself. She is a very sad and lonely buffalo.

One morning, Chip finds an open gate and a chance to get out of the field. She quickly trots down the dirt road to the country store. The fully grown buffalo goes to the front of the building and looks through the glass doors. Then she follows a nervous customer as he dashes to his car. The store parking lot is just no place for a big and friendly buffalo. Once again, Chip has to go back to the field where she belongs.

Every day, Bud takes his jeep and bounces down the rough road to the field. Chip is always eager to see him and waits at the gate. She snorts and paws the ground as the familiar sound of the jeep nears the field.

Bud carries a bucket of pellets for Chip in his jeep. She puts her nose inside the open window. Then she sticks out her rough tongue and licks the yummy pellets into her mouth. Sometimes Chip goes to both sides of the jeep trying to get more pellets. Passengers in the vehicle often scream and bounce to the back seat when the big buffalo comes too close. Bud stays in the jeep while he feeds her. "It's best to use caution around buffalo," he says. "You never know what an excited one might do."

One day when Bud goes to the field, Chip is not waiting at the gate. He is worried and anxious to find his favorite buffalo. Bud shifts the jeep into high gear and roars into the field looking for her. A sharp turn tips over the bucket, and pellets scatter; but he keeps going. He drives past the old cherry orchard that Grandad planted. It is full of bluebirds. "Tru-al-ly, tru-al-ly," the bright bluebirds cheer, but there are no buffalo in the orchard.

Bud can see a cloud of dust near the creek and he follows it to find his buffalo. The bearded animals watch the jeep come to a screeching stop. There is one buffalo walking toward him. "I sure hope that's Chip," he says with a worried look on his face. Sure enough, it is his pet coming for some pellets. She quickly munches down the pellets and follows the jeep back to the gate. After a few grunts of *uh-uh*, she turns and runs back to the herd. "Maybe Chip has finally decided the other buffalo are not so bad after all," says Bud.

19

Chip likes to dust herself in a wallow. It is her favorite place in the field. She digs a pit with her feet and rolls around in the dirt or mud. She dusts herself to keep the flies and bugs away and perhaps to absorb the minerals. One thing is certain: she makes a big cloud of dust when the ground is dry.

The winter days are getting colder. The north wind blows snow across the frozen ground. Chip has grown a thick wooly coat to keep her warm. Now Bud feeds the buffalo bales of hay every day. Chip likes to follow behind the tractor as it scatters out the bales.

The sweet, strong smell of the hay makes her hungry. Several bald eagles are sitting in the tall trees near the buffalo field. The huge birds swoop down and catch mice that crawl out of the hay as Chip eats.

A couple of buffalo start to fight over the hay. They use their heads and strong leg muscles to shove each other around. Each animal pushes with a powerful force, but no one wins. Chip is smart and stays away from the pushy buffalo that like to fight.

Chip was born with little bumps for horns. Her horns sprout upward and become larger as she grows. One winter day, Chip discovers the horns on her head. She uses them like a pitchfork to toss the hay around. Some buffalo break off their horns during a fight. Some have them removed by ranchers for safety reasons. "I'm going to leave the horns on Chip," Bud decides. "She would look odd without them."

Chip sometimes leaves the herd and wanders off by herself. One snowy December day, she goes across the field and through the fence to the neighbors. Their yard glows brightly with Christmas lights strung neatly around the juniper trees. She starts to rub her snow-covered head on the tree next to the house. Sophie hears something outside and opens the door. "It's a buffalo!" She shouts, "Shoo, shoo!"

Chip spooks and catches a cord of Christmas lights in her horns. She takes off in a gallop, dragging the lights behind her. Sophie will never forget the sight of her lights disappearing with the buffalo into the wintery fog.

Slowly, the weather turns warmer again. One by one, the bald eagles leave the field and fly north. Gradually, Chip sheds her winter coat. The wooly brown hair slips off her hide in patches. "Shedding is a sure sign that spring will come soon," says Clint when he sees the shaggy-haired Chip.

Once again, it is spring. The meadowlark sings from a fence post in the meadow. The killdeer eats insects in the plowed field. The bluebird builds a nest in the old cherry tree. Bud apologizes to Sophie and gives her a new box of lights for next Christmas. And it is calving time for the buffalo. Bud sees a buffalo cow all alone at the top of a hill. It is Chip with her first newborn baby. The protective mother stays right beside her little red-haired calf.

Facts about Buffalo

- Buffalo is a more common name for bison.

- Native Americans thanked the Creator for the buffalo.

- Babies are born in late April or May. Buffalo live to be 20-40 years old.

- Baby buffalo weigh 30-70 pounds when born. Cows weigh about 1,000 pounds. Bulls weigh about 2,000 pounds (around a ton). Buffalo stand 5-6 feet tall.

- It takes 8 years for a bull to become fully grown. Bulls usually stay alone. Cows and young bulls stay in herds of 20-50 animals. Cows lead the herds.

- Buffalo can run up to 35 mph. Buffalo can run for a long time.

- Buffalo eat grass, hay, and small bushes. Like beef cattle, they have three stomachs.

- Buffalo signal their moods with their tails. When the tail is up like a flag, watch out!

- Buffalo have poor eyesight, but they have good hearing and sense of smell.

- Buffalo like to wallow.

- Both bulls and cows have upward-curved horns.

- All buffalo have beards.

- Buffalo shed their hair every spring.

Facts about Montana

State Bird
The meadowlark is a grassland bird. Both males and females have yellow breasts. The male spends several hours a day singing from a post. The female works to build a waterproof nest on the ground.

State Flower
The bitterroot has a pink blossom  with delicate shadings. It grows close to the dry ground and blooms about the middle of June.

State Nickname
The Treasure State (because of its gold, silver, and copper).

Size
Montana is the fourth largest state. It takes about 12 hours to drive across the state, going from east to west.

State Tree
The ponderosa pine grows on dry flatland and slopes, and is often surrounded by juniper and sagebrush. Its needles are 5–10 inches long and the cones are 3–6 inches long. These trees can live up to 125 years.

State Agriculture
Cattle and wheat are the leading agricultural products.

State Industry
Mining, tourism, and wood products are the leading industries.

Buffalo Sites
- National Bison Range
- Yellowstone National Park
- Private ranches